a foreigner's conception

Toho Publishing Chapbook Series I

Caroline Furr

TOHO
PUBLISHING

All rights reserved. Published by Toho Publishing LLC,
Philadelphia, in 2020.

FIRST EDITION

Cover design by Josh Martin
Cover art by Caroline Furr
Original layout design by Andrés Cruciani

Series editor: Sean Hanrahan

ISBN 978-1-7336575-7-0 (paperback)

www.tohopub.com

to my husband
Leo Robinson
for the golden gifts of
space and time

Contents

how to measure a whale

tie them with rows of bows
pearls too will oblige the whale
to remain chained

ripeness comes in fall therefore
measuring an unripe whale
is no measure at all
they grow and do become quite large
so a premature investigation is unwise
especially round the toes and eyes
those grow and long too
those toes become as long as their nose
not to mention the expanding condition
of the knees which will appear
look closely - beneath some fleas

some indication they are ready
brown spots close to the stem
or at the back of their necks
pay attention there
and in their hair as those parts turn ruddy
when lying in the muddy
warming in the sun asleep

sly eyes closed
approach now the louche whale
with your pre-trained snail

and let the little one glide
silently from end to end

careful not to wake the blob
so avoid the mob
the snail will help you know the rest
whilst you count his tiny steps

six points—big and small

stars and insects with their six points of contact
touching what is thought of as our world
ever so lightly—it's rightly

stars may explode which is surely dramatic
but bugs who are antic can peep and hide too
even those close by you can't even see
but try

study for comparison those wandering ones
some scuttle on the stairs here and there
others without any borders in faraway corners

cornice—a horizontal projection

if politics displays itself in architecture
so gender might

say words
for she has it all
form and function
with a balustrade along the top
flying buttresses
nooks and crannies

she creates a hasp
by erupting from beneath
and puts a roof over the sky

puffy pink penumbra
disguised as a girl

dear Mr. Olmec

how are ye now—must be plenty old is what we'd say
could be that's why ye have that face which currently
      is out of place
even with your feathered cap you look as though
you've had a slap
and need a nap

if you had words they didn't keep
even to see a neck we'd need to dig deep—how about
      some feet
or is it just those colossal boulders
without even shoulders

where are the womenfolk who'd never scowl in a
      lacey cloak
with hair in curls maybe some pearls
sweet feet in sandals
were they misplaced or rescued by vandals

as a message you're clear that we had something
      to fear
stones don't frown on their own
they weren't that way till you came along

of course your rubber balls decayed
so they have nothing to say
if it was a headache you tried to evade
then we bet you feel entirely betrayed

ode to a statue

we knew you were from Italy
land of fast cars and sewing machines
a place with principles on position and momentum

Plank's Law stood on its wave to see you better
when they brought you down on the barge
it may have been just moviemaking
but such a lush country
with its dells and waterfall surprises
the excellent public transportation
truly merits tribute

and you
you've made a prayer mat of the aurora borealis
and given birth to modern luggage
you can rest now

fearful symmetry

the godfather was a collector of coins and once
on the child's tenth birthday
made him a present of a large bronze

one side was engraved with an image
of two stags their giant antlers
intertwined to form his three initials

and on the other side was their coat of arms
floating midair over a landscape
shielding—as it was—the child and
the old man's natural fear of symmetry

the couple at home

there must have been a fire
some repellent smell that brought her down
to the kitchen and there he was with a big flame
and meat all around—another of his greasy experiments
this time the frying of hocks no doubt personally cut
from an unpleasant ox
her tongue burns with peevish words to say but
glances again at the—no, it was a buffalo—and goes
next he is in the hall his cheek against
the flower-papered wall with a pan in his hand
in her sweetest voice she says
i've worn you out and
been indiscreet with my distaste for meat
glazing and braising he replies and dies
later she finds a note in his coat 'buy dog food'
which they had never owned

> attic red and basement blue
> he had the same hairdo as you
> greeks wore pleats and
> reclined on low couches
> our spouses slouch close to the tv
> with a chablis
> the sofa that was mentioned earlier
> she returns to now—a brocade cage
> with a meat dish in hand
> in memory of the man

mislaid matrimony

we are told good shepherds lie in pastures
and who could refrain such a green terrain
Venus hung just waiting to be picked
but figs were instead

oh shepherds excel
in the inevitable wear and tear of air

now fully grown
perch at the perfect point
to pluck it here

familial

the newspaper said he'd been hacked
but it couldn't have been with an axe
for he wasn't in pieces—he still held his thesis
and his suit was completely intact

there was a small crack round his ears
with a string which led to a brook
and in it we found his mother's blue gown
floating ever so slowly downstream
we pulled it out to dry on the bank
but it stank—so we tossed it back in
which may have seemed mean
but it certainly wasn't obscene

the son lied until the mother cried
then took a short nap in her lap
drank some soup then ran off
with some nameless troupe

this all seems entirely deranged
until you recall the genesis
of the first sentences
it's just another old game

Little Known Facts

Buddha first appears in the Egyptian style, flat
and slanted backwards, his four fragile hairs in an
invisible ponytail. He is always with his mother who
is round and frontal with what appears to be a sofa
for breasts. Not two, but one and from that time in
the sixties, when the Italians were making all their
furniture from huge globs of foam, low to the floor
with unseen legs. She showed only boots with a tent-
like dress covering the entire mess.

     We understand that none of these
descriptions is what you might expect. Nonetheless
true is true as blue is blue and only a nasty rat would
deny these facts.

     Mother did indulge him, he was her one and
all and she prayed daily for luxuriant hair which soon
did appear everywhere in the color red except upon
his face and head. The boy was always at horseplay
and since he was unable to adapt to the lotus
position, she allowed him to spend afternoons at the
cinema where he could sit in comfort.

     Then after all the films had been memorized
his new entertainment was reclusive wandering, it
was more his thing, and she bought him a pretty ring.

Towering incontinence ceased those ways and sent
him home, since he could no longer roam, she bought
him a throne.

A woman, much older it is said, then spied
him upon his lovely velvet throne wearing his
ring and thought him a king. So she proposed and
proposed until Mother finally said, "Yes."

A wife would know a false beard, a foreigner
could only guess.

the artist's day

yesterday all indications of place were painted out
even the glints of reflected sun on the river
that well-placed jewelry thought so convincing
all gone

before us now in this mottled haze floats abstraction
whose crown was color but now has a peewee squeak
with nothing to say

perhaps an escape to the old world is in order and
could be displayed with a morality play

there is a faint outline of a word
set among the drape of half-painted trees
which acts as the exit sign in a theatre—a path
not an obligation

tomorrow your duty is to make another sign
something with sharp cutouts
that hurts their shy eyes and makes them cry

no exit

a window opens at noon
the fauves arrive and spring through
surprised they were to see
it was round all around
and high up and down
with a perspective only they knew
bright shards of red
went to their heads
and blue was no glue
so their plans run aground
their exit defective
there's no way to conclude
without a big feud
when cubism arrives
to inhabit twin facets
that morph in boxes
brown boxes   (oh no)
they're harassed anew
so yield back to blue
it may seem a circle to you
another pursuit to execute
but they find fascination
in this strange vocation
so it's best to let them be
to do whatever it is they do

when Auden spoke

what did he say and when he wrote
what did he write concerning
the preliminary sensation of a swift
arrow to the back of the head
dispensing fluid cool to the brain

surely more punctuation than this

he came over long ago
and nailed the place
knew what plains and spiders meant
how to get around and out

we didn't pay attention though
stuck around we did

reinventing fire
and the little grandpappy wheel

abundance

a holiday platter is arranged thus
with the tail plumage allowed to drape over the side
peasants and pheasants hate it
when those parts are removed (in fact en fin)
keep it all intact and serve the cow hooves up
tongue hanging out close to the plate
of your favorite mate at the table

if you are able this is what can be achieved
by too much—your guest's delight
will be great so never hesitate to use
the storm drain racks you've stored
in the basement as placemats

animation

say the word éclair
then retrieve a happy word that is not hair
the thing itself is not a chair that can sit forever
without spoiling and attracting ants
that would stick to your pants

if you would chance upon a chair with a resting éclair
would you care
or despair and pretend to be debonair

you dear antique
we know you have mystique—but speak
or send us a letter with the word we seek
perhaps a little note
write it here on the side of this small goat

and never fear to jump or shout
your word is not the end of what you are about

nudes descending

the lines of our bodies are irrelevant
we were beauty on the bois
teenagers in love

dash
confidence
movement all

ridiculous tiny terriers in
inverse proportion to the world

a more modern mermaid
more ancient knight

deep-sea divers

one fish
two fish

leaving Texas

you heard the sighing sounds
when the overhanging willows
brushed their wings
but listen closer now
as the swans pass by again
with clear instructions
you will not return to this place
where a false embrace of duty
no longer waits
with your back against the wall
place your horns at your feet
and wrapped in tattered rags
take your broom and sweep
toward the fork in the road
on the journey west
open the shutters of the desert
to view snowfall over
a subterranean pool where
there are singing people in boats
and on the bank
a boat for you

pioneering

that cane—that crutch
only add to your appeal

so your scarf
what does that hide that she wants to know
see and touch

evergreen timber defined an outpost
and the tangled meeting

the net too closed a space
was it a meadow or just a scrap of dirty lace

deep into the wood forming a bracket
it has turned to night now and we see better
as they stack it up together against bad weather

typical day

he'd been under the protection
of inflated draperies
even though he wasn't a statue
nor an insane patient
his outlook was more urbane

nevertheless
the lampshades did catch fire
when he switched off the lights
so often that the only illumination
was from the pigeon in the kitchen

mired in some roundelay
with nothing cooking in the oven
unable to govern the locks
the flocks arrived
to reset the clocks

exhausted and weeping
he leaves off his sweeping
bids goodnight to the pigeon
and takes to his bed
it was a perfect day—he said

incessant strumming

you could get lucky if you'd lose the guitar
put them in jelly jars and send them to mars
in boxcars

that moan you hear is not my hormone
but the drone of your strumming

while i'm humming you sit on your headstone
with your cigars and sitar
if you'd only cease you could be my beast

parting words

formless herself

she creates her frame

by abducting a shadow

> *wet and thick*
> *the plumbing drips*
> *tick-tock tick-tock*
> *it's all damn lies*
> *the frig replies*

at last jewelry night is here

an invitation-only event

with more hearts to break
but then it's dry leftover cake

About the Poet

Caroline Furr is a visual artist.

This is her first voyage out

in the fragile boat made of words.

Born in Oklahoma, she has lived and worked
in Texas, Los Angeles, Barcelona. And now
Philadelphia.

There is more at carolinefurr.com.